Novels for Students, Volume 41

Project Editor: Sara Constantakis Rights Acquisition and Management: Mary Snell, Robyn Young Composition: Evi Abou-El-Seoud Manufacturing: Rhonda Dover

Imaging: John Watkins

Product Design: Pamela A. E. Galbreath, Jennifer Wahi Content Conversion: Katrina Coach Product Manager: Meggin Condino © 2013 Gale, Cengage Learning

For product information and technology assistance, contact us at **Gale Customer Support, 1-800-877-4253.**

For permission to use material from this text or product, submit all requests online at **www.cengage.com/permissions**.

Further permissions questions can be emailed to **permissionrequest@cengage.com** While every effort has been made to ensure the reliability of the information presented in this publication, Gale, a part of Cengage Learning, does not guarantee the accuracy of the data contained herein. Gale accepts no payment for listing; and inclusion in the publication of any organization, agency, institution, publication, service, or individual does not imply endorsement of the editors or publisher. Errors brought to the attention of the publisher and verified to the satisfaction of the publisher will be corrected in future editions.

Gale
27500 Drake Rd.
Farmington Hills, MI, 48331-3535

ISBN-13: 978-1-4144-9484-5
ISBN-10: 1-4144-9484-X
ISSN 1094-3552

This title is also available as an e-book.

ISBN-13: 978-1-4144-9270-4
ISBN-10: 1-4144-9270-7
Contact your Gale, a part of Cengage Learning sales
representative for ordering information.

Printed in Mexico
1 2 3 4 5 6 7 16 15 14 13 12

Bleak House

Charles Dickens 1852-1853

Introduction

Bleak House, a novel by Charles Dickens, was first published in installments from 1852 to 1853. It was extremely popular with readers, with each part selling about thirty-five thousand copies. In 1853, it was bound into one volume and published in America by Harper. Many modern critics consider it to be Dickens's finest novel. *Bleak House* has several plotlines. One is a legal case regarding the settlement of a will that has dragged on for more years than anyone can remember and shows no sign of being settled. A second is an unfolding mystery and detective story surrounding the aristocratic

Lady Dedlock and an anonymous copier of law documents. A third is the story of Esther Summerson, told by Esther in the first person as she lives at Bleak House in the care of her guardian. The plotlines all intersect and give Dickens many opportunities for satire that attacks the failure of England's social institutions to perform the tasks they are designed to do. He takes aim at the long delays of the legal system, the inability of Parliament to address the needs of the poor, the misguided efforts of philanthropists who do not understand the real needs of people, and the unsanitary, disease-ridden conditions in England's capital city. *Bleak House* treats a broad swath of English society, from aristocratic houses to the slums and many points in between. It contains a typical Dickensian gallery of memorable characters, both noble and ignoble, and ample amounts of comedy and tragedy.

Author Biography

One of England's greatest novelists, Charles Dickens was born in Landport, near Portsmouth, Hampshire, on February 7, 1812, the second of eight children of John Dickens and Elizabeth Barrow. John Dickens was a clerk in the Navy Pay Office. When Dickens was twelve, his father got into financial difficulties and was imprisoned for debt in Marshalsea Prison. The young Dickens was sent to work for several months in a shoe-blacking warehouse, thus interrupting his education and giving him a lifelong sympathy for the plight of child laborers. Several years later, Dickens became a solicitor's clerk and then a court reporter. In 1832, he was a reporter for an evening newspaper, and he later became a reporter for the *Morning Chronicle*.

Dickens's first short story was published in a magazine in 1833, and in 1836 he published his descriptions of London life, *Sketches by Boz*, which were inspired by his journalistic work. In that year he also became the editor of a new magazine, *Bentley's Miscellany*, and married Catherine Hogarth, the daughter of the editor of the *Evening Chronicle*. They had ten children but separated in 1858.

Dickens's first novel was *The Pickwick Papers* (1836-37), which, like most of his fiction, was published in installments in magazines. The success of this novel encouraged Dickens to continue, and within the next few years he wrote *Oliver Twist* (1837-39), *Nicholas Nickleby* (1838-39), *The Old Curiosity Shop* (1840-41), and *Barnaby Rudge* (1841). His work was enormously popular in both England and the United States, and he embarked on his first trip to the United States and Canada in 1842, speaking out in favor of the abolition of slavery. *American Notes* (1842) and *Martin Chuzzlewit* (1843-44) were the direct result of his American tour.

During the 1840s and 1850s, Dickens continued to publish at a prodigious rate. *A Christmas Carol* (1843), *Dombey and Son* (1846-48), *David Copperfield* (1849-50), *Bleak House* (1852-53), *Hard Times* (1854), *Little Dorrit* (1855-57), and *A Tale of Two Cities* (1859) all appeared during this period. Dickens was also the editor of *Household Words*, a magazine he founded in 1850. When that magazine ceased publication in 1859, he became editor of a new magazine, *All the Year Round*.

Dickens continued to enjoy great popularity, and in the 1850s and 1860s he traveled around England, Scotland, and Ireland giving highly successful public readings from his novels. He also gave a reading in Paris in 1863 and went on a reading tour of the east coast of the United States for four months from 1867 to 1868.

During the 1860s, Dickens was frequently in poor health, but he continued to take on new work and reading engagements. *Great Expectations* (1860-61) and *Our Mutual Friend* (1864-65) were the products of the final decade of his life. In 1870, Dickens was working on *The Mystery of Edwin Drood*, which had begun publication but remained unfinished, when he had a stroke. He died at the age of fifty-eight, at Gadshill, near Rochester, Kent, on June 9, 1870.

Chapters I-VI

Bleak House begins on a foggy day in London, probably in the 1840s. The fog is at its densest at the Court of Chancery, where legal cases drag on for years without resolution. In particular, the case of Jarndyce and Jarndyce has gone on for generations and is so complex that not even the lawyers understand it. It is legendary for its length and its costs, both human and monetary. This day, two young people who are wards of the court in the Jarndyce case are applying to live with their cousin, John Jarndyce.

Chapter II takes place in the London home of Lady Dedlock and her husband, Sir Leicester Dedlock. They receive a visit from their lawyer, Mr. Tulkinghorn, about the Jarndyce suit, in which Lady Dedlock has an interest. She is startled by the handwriting in one of the documents the lawyer shows her.

Chapter III introduces Esther Summerson, who tells of her deprived early life when she was raised by her aunt, Miss Barbary, in Windsor. After Miss Barbary dies when Esther is fourteen, Esther is told that Mr. John Jarndyce wants to provide for her education and is now her guardian. Esther teaches school for six years in Reading. Then she goes to London, where she meets the two wards in the

Jarndyce case, Ada Clare and Richard Carstone. They all are sent to live with John Jarndyce at Bleak House in Hertfordshire.

In chapter IV, before they go to Bleak House, they stay the night with Mrs. Jellyby, a philanthropist who devotes herself to the betterment of Africa, neglecting her husband and seven children. The following day (chapter V) the three young people visit the Krook Rag and Bottle Warehouse near the Chancery. The owner, Krook, tells them that one of the suitors in the Jarndyce case, Tom Jarndyce, shot himself out of frustration because the case had dragged on so long. Later (chapter VI), the young people go to Bleak House, where they meet their guardian and cousin, Jarndyce. At dinner they meet Harold Skimpole, a charming, childlike man who expects others to look after him. Later that night, Skimpole is saved from being arrested for debt by Esther and Richard, who pay the debt for him.

Chapters VII-XII

In chapter VII, the narrative turns to the Dedlocks' estate in Chesney Wold, Lincolnshire. The old housekeeper, Mrs. Rouncewell, is there with her grandson, who has taken a fancy to Rosa, one of the maids. Mr. Guppy, a junior law clerk from London, arrives with a friend, wanting to take a tour of the house. He is fascinated when he sees a portrait of Lady Dedlock. Her face is familiar to him, but he does not know why.

In chapter VIII, Jarndyce explains the Chancery suit to Esther. It began with a will made by one of the rich Jarndyces. The dispute is over how the trusts named in the will are to be administered. Jarndyce explains the misery the case has inflicted on everyone. Esther is entrusted with the management of the house. One day Mrs. Pardiggle, a do-gooder like Mrs. Jellyby, visits Bleak House with her five young sons, whom she compels to donate their weekly allowances to worthy causes. Esther and Ada accompany Mrs. Pardiggle to the house of a poor brickmaker, where she lectures the family.

Media Adaptations

- *Bleak House* was adapted for television, starring Gillian Anderson, Alun Armstrong, and Charlie Brooks, and issued on DVD in 2006 by BBC Warner. Running time is 465 minutes. This was a very successful adaptation. It is split up into half-hour episodes, each one ending with a cliffhanger.

- An earlier adaptation, starring Diana Rigg, Denholm Elliott, Philip Franks, T. P. McKenna, and Brian Deacon, and directed by Ross Devenish, was made in 1985 by BBC Warner and was released on DVD in 2005. Running time is 418 minutes.

- Several versions have been released on audio CDs. In 2007, Blackstone Audio released an unabridged edition.

- In 2003, Universal released an audiobook version read by Terje Rypdal.

- In 2003, Penguin Audiobooks released a version with Beatie Edney and Ronald Pickup as narrators.

- A 1986 version, read by Sir John Gielgud, is available on audiocassette, published by Newman Communications.

Richard and Ada fall in love (chapter IX), and Jarndyce is visited by an old friend, the quarrelsome but kind Lawrence Boythorn, who is in a dispute with Sir Leicester about a right-of-way between their properties. Guppy arrives with papers for Boythorn. Alone with Esther, he proposes to her, but she rejects his proposal immediately.

In chapter X, Mr. Tulkinghorn goes to the law-stationer's shop near Chancery Lane run by Mr. and Mrs. Snagsby. Tulkinghorn wants to know the name of the law copier who copied the Jarndyce document he carries with him. Snagsby tells him that the clerk's name is Nemo. Tulkinghorn visits Nemo at his lodgings at Krook's but finds him dead from an opium overdose. An inquest takes place in chapter XI. No one knows much about Nemo, and the verdict is accidental death. In chapter XII, the Dedlocks return from Paris and are visited by Tulkinghorn. Tulkinghorn informs Lady Dedlock that the writer of the document she inquired about is dead. This news distresses her. She and Tulkinghorn are suspicious of each other.

Chapters XIII-XVIII

Richard needs to find an occupation. He impulsively decides to become a surgeon and is apprenticed to Bayham Badger in Chelsea. Love-sick Guppy makes a nuisance of himself by following Esther around, and Ada tells Esther that she and Richard are in love. Jarndyce says they must wait until Richard is established in a profession.

In chapter XIV, Esther and Ada meet Caddy, Mrs. Jellyby's oldest child, who is planning to elope and marry a dancing teacher, Prince Turveydrop. Esther meets Prince and his vain father at the dance academy and then with Jarndyce visits one of the lodgers at Krook's, the eccentric Miss Flite. Esther also encounters a young doctor, Mr. Woodcourt.

Chapter XV follows Jarndyce as he tries to help the orphaned children of Neckett, the sheriff's officer who had tried to arrest Skimpole for debt and who has just died. The oldest child, thirteen-year-old Charley, is looking after the others so they will not be sent to the orphanage.

In chapter XVI, an unnamed woman in a veil (clearly Lady Dedlock) goes to the slum district in London known as Tom-all-Alone's. There she seeks out Jo, a boy who knew Nemo, the dead law copyist. She gets Jo to take her to where Nemo lived, died, and was buried.

Esther narrates chapter XVII. Unsuited to becoming a doctor, Richard goes into law instead so he can follow the Jarndyce case. Jarndyce tells Esther what he knows about her origins; he does not know who her parents are. Woodcourt informs them he is to become a ship's surgeon and will be away for a long time.

In chapter XVIII, the residents of Bleak House visit Boythorn, and at church, Esther sees Lady Dedlock for the first time. The aristocratic woman reminds Esther of her aunt and her childhood, but she does not know why. Later, on the Dedlock estate, Lady Dedlock is introduced to Esther and looks quickly away as if in dislike.

Chapters XIX-XXIV

Mr. and Mrs. Snagsby entertain Mr. Chadband, a minister, and his wife for tea. A constable brings in Jo, who is suspected of stealing. Jo says a lady gave him the money. Guppy questions the boy, wanting to put the pieces of the puzzle together. He also hears Mrs. Chadband speak of her time as housekeeper for Miss Barbary, Esther's aunt.

In chapter XX, Guppy wants to spy on Krook and arranges for his friend Jobling to lodge in the room formerly occupied by Nemo.

Chapter XXI is devoted to the humorless Smallweed family. The grandfather is a moneylender. An old soldier, Mr. George, who has borrowed money, visits. Smallweed threatens him with unpleasant consequences should he be late in repaying it. George mentions that Smallwood and his moneylending associates tricked his friend, Captain Hawdon.

In chapter XXII, Tulkinghorn is investigating a connection between Lady Dedlock and Nemo. He sends Inspector Bucket and Mr. Snagsby to the slums to find the boy, Jo. When they return to Tulkinghorn with Jo, a veiled lady is there. Jo at first identifies her as the lady who gave him the money, but then when he sees her hand and hears her voice, he says it is not her. The lady is Lady Dedlock's maid, Hortense, whose clothes Lady Dedlock had borrowed.

Chapter XXIII returns to Esther's narration.

Richard is in debt and is foolishly putting his faith in the Jarndyce suit. He wants to join the army. Esther visits Caddy Jellyby and helps her tell Prince's father that she and Prince are engaged. Mr. Turveydrop at first opposes the engagement but then gives the couple his blessing.

In chapter XXIV, Richard is given an army commission and is to serve in Ireland. Jarndyce asks him to break off his engagement to Ada, since he is not showing much responsibility. This leads to an estrangement between Richard and Jarndyce. The Jarndyce case drags on, and the slowness of the law claims another victim, a Mr. Gridley, who has been in a long battle with Chancery.

Chapters XXV-XXX

Mrs. Snagsby notices a change in her husband, who has been asked by Bucket to keep the incident involving Jo secret. Mrs. Snagsby suspects her husband has been up to no good, even thinking that Jo must be his son.

Chapter XXVI shows Mr. George at the shooting gallery he owns, with his assistant, Phil. Smallweed arrives and asks about Captain Hawdon, George's friend, saying that he does not believe Hawdon is dead. He adds that a lawyer friend of his (Tulkinghorn) would pay George to produce a letter with Hawdon's handwriting on it. Smallweed and George go to Tulkinghorn's chamber (chapter XXVII), where Tulkinghorn asks George for the handwriting sample. George refuses, and also insists that Hawdon is dead. George visits his friends the Bagnets for advice and returns to Tulkinghorn, still refusing to hand over the requested sample.

In chapter XXVIII, the Dedlocks receive Mrs. Rouncewell's son, an ironmaster who is standing for Parliament. Mr. Rouncewell asks permission for his son Watt to marry the Dedlocks' maid, Rosa. Sir Leicester, conscious that the ironmaster is his social inferior, says they will allow the girl to make up her own mind.

In chapter XXIX, Guppy visits Lady Dedlock and mentions the resemblance between Lady Dedlock and Esther. His aim is to find out about the circumstances of Esther's birth because he wants to marry her. He has found out that Esther's name was Esther Hawdon, not Summerson. Explaining further, Guppy says that the dead Nemo was Captain Hawdon and that he knows Lady Dedlock went to visit his grave. He adds that Hawdon left a collection of letters, which Guppy can bring to her if she wishes. Lady Dedlock is stunned by this news. Esther is her child. Her sister, Miss Barbary, had told her the baby had died but had secretly taken her and raised her.

In chapter XXX, Esther receives a visit from Mr. Woodcourt's mother, who says her son is restricted in his choice of a wife because of the distinguished family he comes from, thus discouraging Esther from having hopes of marrying him. Esther attends Caddy's wedding.

Chapters XXXI-XXXVI

Esther and her new maid, Charley, get called to a cottage in St. Albans, where they find Jo. The sick boy was found on the street. Esther takes him home, and Jarndyce agrees that he should stay the night. However, in the morning, Jo has vanished. Charley gets sick with smallpox, caught from Jo, and she infects Esther. Charley recovers, but Esther goes blind.

Chapter XXXII returns to Guppy. Krook has agreed to show Hawdon's letters to him and Weevle (the name used by Jobling). When they go to Krook's room, all they find are charred clothes and ashes. Krook has literally gone up in smoke, a case of spontaneous combustion.

In chapter XXXIII, Guppy wants Weevle to stay on at Krook's so he can get his hands on all of Krook's papers. But Smallweed turns up and announces that Krook was Mrs. Smallweed's brother. He takes possession of the shop. Guppy has to tell Lady Dedlock that he cannot, after all, produce the letters he promised her, because they perished with Krook.

In the next chapter, Smallweed demands from George payment of a debt, for which George's friend Mr. Bagnet is a cosigner. George and Bagnet ask Smallweed for more time, but Smallweed just sends them to his lawyer, Tulkinghorn. George gets out of the bad situation when he agrees to show Tulkinghorn a letter from Captain Hawdon.

Chapter XXXV returns to Esther's narrative. She recovers her sight but her face is scarred. She learns from Jarndyce that Richard has turned hostile to him. Miss Flite comes to visit and tells Esther her story. All her family have been ruined by the Jarndyce lawsuit. Miss Flite also informs Esther that Woodcourt was in a shipwreck and became a hero by saving others.

In chapter XXXVI, Esther and Charley stay at Boythorn's house. Esther meets Lady Dedlock, who admits she is Esther's mother. She says she did not know Esther had survived. She tells Esther that this is the only time they are to meet and that Esther must keep her secret. Esther forgives her.

Chapters XXXVII-XLII

Richard, still hoping to get rich from the Jarndyce case, visits Esther. He thinks Jarndyce is working against his interests. Esther tries to reason with him, to no avail.

In chapter XXXVIII, Esther visits Caddy Turveydrop, who is now happily married. They visit Guppy, who thinks Esther is coming round to accepting his proposal. But when she raises her veil and he sees her disfigured face, he wants to escape any commitment to her. She asks him to cease his pursuit into her affairs, and he agrees.

In the next chapter, Richard visits his lawyer, Vholes, who says that progress is being made in the Jarndyce case. He also says that Jarndyce is working against Richard's interests, which is what

Richard wants to hear. Guppy and Jobling go to the shop formerly owned by Krook to collect Jobling's belongings. The Smallweeds are there, going through Krook's possessions, and Tulkinghorn is there also, secretly seeking the missing letters from Lady Dedlock to Hawdon.

Chapter XL tells of the general election in England. Sir Leicester loses control of two parliamentary seats he had controlled to the opposition party, which is supported by Mr. Rouncewell and his son. Tulkinghorn tells a story in the presence of Lady Dedlock that is clearly Lady Dedlock's own, although he disguises the details. Now Lady Dedlock knows that Tulkinghorn knows about her past.

In chapter XLI, Lady Dedlock confronts Tulkinghorn, saying that she is willing to sign any document that would help her husband. She plans to leave Chesney Wold that night. Tulkinghorn tells her not to. For the time being, he intends to keep her secret because he is mindful of the honor of Sir Leicester and the family reputation.

Tulkinghorn returns to London (chapter XLII), where he is confronted by an angry Hortense, the French maid who has been fired by Lady Dedlock. Tulkinghorn has been using her to ensnare Lady Dedlock. Hortense demands that the lawyer either find her new employment or use her to destroy Lady Dedlock.

Chapters XLIII-XLVIII

Esther, Ada, and Mr. Jarndyce ask Skimpole not to take money from Richard. Sir Leicester invites the Bleak House residents to visit Chesney Wold, which makes Esther realize she must confess her secret about her mother to her guardian to prevent such a situation arising. When he hears Esther's story, Jarndyce is kind to her.

In chapter XLIV, Esther and Jarndyce discuss Lady Dedlock's precarious situation, with Tulkinghorn and Hortense wanting to bring her down. Jarndyce writes a letter to Esther, asking her to marry him. She does not reply for two weeks, at which point she accepts his proposal, putting her feelings for Woodcourt to rest.

In chapter XLV, Vholes, Richard's lawyer, visits Bleak House and says that Richard is in debt and will lose his army commission. Esther visits Richard at his barracks in Deal, Kent. Richard says it is too late, but anyway, he does not like being a soldier. He is obsessed with the Chancery suit. As Esther leaves, she encounters Woodcourt and asks him to befriend Richard in London.

The next two chapters (XLVI and XLVII) focus on the fate of the poor boy, Jo. Woodcourt encounters Jo in the slum of Tom-all-Alone's. Jo is still sick, and Woodcourt arranges for George at the shooting gallery to take him in. George tells Woodcourt that Tulkinghorn has a hold over him and may evict him from the gallery. Jo feels guilty because he made Esther sick, and he hopes he can be forgiven. Despite Woodcourt's efforts, Jo dies.

In chapter XLVIII, Lady Dedlock tells Rosa, her maid, that she is sending her away so that she can be with the young man who is courting her. When Lady Dedlock tells her husband of her intentions, Tulkinghorn is there also. Then in private, Tulkinghorn tells Lady Dedlock he will expose her secret because she has broken their agreement by trying to protect Rosa from the shame of being associated with her. Later, Tulkinghorn is shot dead in his own house.

Chapters XLIX-LIV

At a birthday party for Mrs. Bagnet, George and Inspector Bucket are in attendance. After a pleasant evening, Bucket and George leave together, and Bucket arrests George for the murder of Tulkinghorn.

Chapter L returns to Esther's narrative. Esther tries to help Caddy, who is unwell and has also given birth to a handicapped child. Woodcourt restores Caddy to health. Esther explains to Ada and Caddy that she is engaged to her guardian. Ada seems to withdraw from Esther after hearing this news.

Woodcourt fulfills his promise to befriend Richard (chapter LI). Ada confesses to Esther that she and Richard have been married for two months and she will henceforth be living with him. Esther is happy for them but sad that she will no longer have Ada living with her at Bleak House.

In chapter LII, Woodcourt, Esther, Mr.

Jarndyce, and later the Bagnets visit George in prison. They all believe he is innocent, but he refuses to hire a lawyer. George tells Esther that on the night of the murder, he saw a woman who resembled Esther, dressed in black, coming down the stairs at Tulkinghorn's house. Mrs. Bagnet sets off to find George's mother.

Chapters LIII and LIV show Inspector Bucket at work, solving the murder case. He has been receiving anonymous letters accusing Lady Dedlock of being the murderess. He tells Sir Leicester the case is almost complete, and he questions Mercury, a footman at the Dedlock townhouse, about when Lady Dedlock went out for a walk on the night of the murder. Bucket tells Sir Leicester about Lady Dedlock's past, including her lover, her child, and her visit to Hawdon's grave. Smallweed arrives, wanting to be paid for the letters from Lady Dedlock to Hawdon that he had found at Krook's and passed on to Tulkinghorn. Bucket then brings in the murderer, Hortense, Lady Dedlock's former maid. Hortense had been lodging at the Buckets' home, and the inspector and his wife collected evidence against her. Sir Leicester is shocked and has a stroke.

Chapters LV-LX

In prison, George is reunited with his mother. Mrs. Rouncewell goes to Lady Dedlock with an anonymous letter accusing Lady Dedlock of the murder. She asks her to help George. Guppy informs Lady Dedlock that her letters to Hawdon have been found. Feeling the net closing in on her, Lady Dedlock writes to her husband, denying the murder but confessing her shame. She leaves the house in the night.

In chapter LVI, the stricken Sir Leicester is nursed by Mrs. Rouncewell. He writes on a slate that he forgives his wife. In Lady Dedlock's room, Bucket finds Esther's handkerchief. This gives him the clue he needs, and he and Esther set off in search of Lady Dedlock. The chase continues in chapter LVII, during a severe snowstorm. In St. Albans, they find that Lady Dedlock was at the house of Jenny, the brickmaker's wife, but left on foot. As the day wears on, Bucket begins to lose hope. Then he thinks he knows what happened, and he and Esther turn back toward London.

In chapter LVIII, Sir Leicester waits, hoping for his wife's return and explaining to everyone that nothing has changed between him and his wife. He still loves her and has no complaint against her.

Esther's narrative continues in chapter LIX. Bucket and Esther reach London and go to the Snagsbys, where they are given a note left by Lady Dedlock when she stopped there to rest. The note says she knows she will die in the streets. Guster, the maid, says that Lady Dedlock asked her for directions to the pauper cemetery (where Nemo was buried). Bucket and Esther, as well as Woodcourt, walk to the cemetery, where they find Lady Dedlock lying dead.

In chapter LX, Esther becomes ill following her mother's death but recovers under Woodcourt's supervision. Woodcourt accepts a position in Yorkshire, arranged for him by Jarndyce. Richard becomes more ill and is still obsessed with the Jarndyce case. His wife Ada is pregnant.

Chapters LXI-LXVII

Esther tells Skimpole not to visit Richard and Ada because he uses their money. Skimpole agrees. Woodcourt walks Esther home and tells her he loves her, but for Esther, honored though she is, it is too late. She is already committed to Jarndyce.

In chapter LXII, Esther and Jarndyce agree to marry next month. Bucket arrives with Smallweed, who has found a will relevant to the Jarndyce case, and it is dated later than the other wills. It favors Richard and Ada. Jarndyce takes the will to a lawyer, Kenge, who says it will settle the case.

Chapter LXIII tells of George's trip to the industrial north, where he visits his brother at one of the latter's iron factories. They have not seen each other for years, and it is a joyful reunion. George is now settled at Chesney Wold, his boyhood home, with his long-lost mother, Mrs. Rouncewell.

In Esther's narrative (chapter LXIV), Esther inspects the house in Yorkshire that Jarndyce has prepared for Woodcourt. It is called Bleak House. Jarndyce tells Esther that he knows she would be happier marrying Woodcourt, and that is what he desires for her. Back in London, Guppy, now a lawyer, makes another marriage proposal to Esther, which Jarndyce rejects on her behalf.

In chapter LXV, the Jarndyce case is finally settled. No one gains anything except the lawyers because all the money is eaten up in costs. The stricken Richard is reconciled to Jarndyce. He acknowledges his mistake and talks about starting over, but he dies as he embraces Ada.

Chapter LXVI reveals that Lady Dedlock is buried in the family vault. The much weakened Sir Leicester is attended by George, Mrs. Rouncewell, and his cousin Volumnia. The Dedlock family is in its final decline.

In the final chapter, Esther reveals that she has been married to Woodcourt for seven years and they have two daughters. Ada has a son, Richard, and they both live with Jarndyce. Woodcourt is respected and loved by the local people, and Esther is also admired.

Bayham Badger

A cousin of Kenge's, Bayham Badger is a surgeon in Chelsea to whom Richard Carstone is apprenticed.

Mrs. Bayham Badger

Mrs. Badger has been married twice before, and she speaks often and with admiration of her former husbands, Captain Swosser and Professor Dingo.

Matthew Bagnet

Bagnet owns a music shop and is an old friend of Mr. George. He defers to his wife in all things. Bagnet is cosigner for a loan George receives from Smallwood and at one point fears he may have to go to prison for debt.

Mrs. Bagnet

Mrs. Bagnet is Matthew's wife. She is described as "strong, busy, active, honest-faced," and it is her intelligence and efficiency that keep the Bagnet household running smoothly. Her husband relies on her.

Bagnet Children

The Bagnet children, Woolwich, Quebec, and Malta, are named after the places where they were born.

Miss Barbary

Miss Barbary is Esther's aunt. She is an unsmiling, highly religious woman who raises Esther in secrecy after telling her sister Honaria (Lady Dedlock) that the baby, born out of wedlock, is dead. Miss Barbary was once in love with Lawrence Boythorn but she abruptly broke off their relationship in order to raise Esther. She tells Esther it would have been better had she never been born.

Mrs. Blinder

Mrs. Blinder is a good-natured old woman who runs a boardinghouse in Bell Yard where Tom Gridley and the Neckett family live. She takes a kindly interest in the welfare of the children.

Lawrence Boythorn

Boythorn is an old friend of John Jarndyce from their school days together. He is a man of violent and extreme opinions, which he always expresses with great force. He is involved in a long-running dispute with his neighbor, Sir Leicester, about a right-of-way between their properties. Despite his fiery temper, however, Boythorn is an amiable, kind, and harmless man, and Esther, Ada, and Richard like him. Boythorn is a bachelor, having been disappointed in love by Miss Barbary.

Inspector Bucket

Inspector Bucket is the detective who solves the Tulkinghorn murder, relying on careful police work and his own instincts. He is a courteous man who understands human nature and often has a certain sympathy for those he has to arrest.

Mrs. Bucket

Mrs. Bucket is enlisted by her husband to help solve the murder by watching Hortense's every move when she stays as a lodger at their house.

Richard Carstone

Richard Carstone is a nineteen-year-old orphan and one of the wards in the Jarndyce case. As a young man he is generous, cheerful, and carefree. He quickly falls in love with Ada Clare when they live together at Bleak House under the guardianship of John Jarndyce. However, Richard does not find his way in life. He decides on impulse to train as a surgeon but quickly gets bored by it. Then he wants to become a lawyer, but only because this can help him get deeply involved in the Chancery suit, which he is convinced is going to make him rich. He starts to get into debt, leaves the law, and joins the army, but he still goes on accumulating debt. He marries

Ada, but it is too late to repair his fortunes. He dies a young man after hearing that he will not after all acquire any money from the suit.

Mr. Chadband

Mr. Chadband is a pompous minister who speaks in high-flown rhetorical language that many regard as nonsense. He singles out the poor boy Jo and tells him he is living in a state of darkness and sin, and that is why he is miserable.

Mrs. Rachel Chadband

Mrs. Chadband, Mr. Chadband's wife, used to be Miss Barbary's housekeeper, and therefore she knows the secret of Esther's origins. She is a severe, mostly silent woman.

Ada Clare

Ada Clare is a seventeen-year-old ward of the court in the Jarndyce case, and she is sent to Bleak House to live with her cousin, John Jarndyce, who serves as her guardian. She and her fellow ward Richard Carstone soon fall in love, and she also forms the closest of friendships with Esther. Ada secretly marries Richard when she comes of age, and she gives birth to his son after his death. Ada is sweet, innocent, and affectionate.

Coavinses

See Mr. Neckett

Lady Dedlock

Lady Dedlock is Sir Leicester's wife. She is twenty years younger than he, and in middle age she is still beautiful, although she has a proud, haughty demeanor. She is also bored with her life and travels between the family estate in Lincolnshire and their townhouse in London without much purpose. She and Sir Leicester have no children. Lady Dedlock has some unstated interest in the Jarndyce case, and she also guards a secret—that she had an illegitimate child with Captain Hawdon before she met Sir Leicester. Piece by piece, the secret comes out, beginning when she reacts noticeably when she sees Hawdon's handwriting on a legal document that Tulkinghorn shows her. When she meets Esther by chance and discovers that Esther is her daughter, she drops her cold manner and embraces Esther with great emotion. She also shows kindness to her maid, Rosa, perhaps seeing her as a substitute daughter. But when her enemy, the lawyer Tulkinghorn, threatens to expose her secret, the net closes in on her. After she realizes that she may also be accused of murdering Tulkinghorn, she leaves a note for her husband and runs away, dying in the snow at the gates of the London cemetery where Hawdon lies.

Sir Leicester Dedlock

Sir Leicester married his much younger wife

out of love, and he continues to love her and treat her with great respect throughout their marriage. Even when he discovers his wife's guilty past, he forgives her completely. Sir Leicester is an aristocrat of the old school. He is proud of his family heritage and believes himself to be an important man. He is very disturbed at the social changes going on in England and is shocked when the two parliamentary seats he is used to controlling are won by the opposition party.

Volumnia Dedlock

Volumnia is Sir Leicester Dedlock's sixty-year-old cousin. A single woman, she lives modestly in Bath on an allowance from Sir Leicester, visiting him at Chesney Wold from time to time. After Sir Leicester's stroke, she nurses him, and she becomes his heir.

Miss Flite

Miss Flite is an eccentric old woman who hopes to gain something from the Jarndyce case. Every day she waits at Chancery for a judgment. In her lodgings at Krook's, she keeps about twenty birds in cages, saying she will release them when the judgment comes.

Mr. George

Mr. George is a fifty-year-old former soldier who runs a shooting gallery. He trains Richard

Carstone. A good-hearted man, he takes in those down on their luck, such as his assistant Phil and the boy Jo. He owes money to Smallweed and is afraid he may be evicted. Mr. George is arrested for the murder of Tulkinghorn, but his innocence is soon established. He is reunited with his mother, Mrs. Rouncewell, and his brother.

Mr. Gridley

Mr. Gridley is a man who is made very angry by a long delay in his legal case at the Court of Chancery. He becomes so belligerent about it that he is cited for contempt of court. He takes refuge at George's shooting gallery, where he dies.

Mr. William Guppy

Mr. Guppy is an ambitious and cunning law clerk at Kenge and Carboy's. He takes a fancy to Esther and proposes to her, but she is not the slightest bit interested. Guppy manages to find out about Lady Dedlock's secret, although he fails in his goal of finding the letters she sent to Hawdon. After he has qualified as a lawyer, he proposes a second time to Esther but is once again turned down.

Guster

Guster is the maid in the Snagsby household. She is clumsy and excitable, given to having fits.

Captain Hawdon

See Nemo

Mademoiselle Hortense

The Frenchwoman Hortense is Lady Dedlock's maid. When Lady Dedlock dismisses her and favors Rosa instead, Hortense is angry and bitter. When Tulkinghorn refuses to help her, she murders him.

John Jarndyce

John Jarndyce is the guardian of his cousins Ada Clare and Richard Carstone, and also of Esther. Jarndyce is a single man of about sixty, and he is always kind and courteous, careful to do the right thing. He is well off financially and offers help to the less fortunate whenever he can, but in a quiet way that is the opposite of the kind of philanthropy offered by loud individuals such as Mrs. Pardiggle and Mrs. Jellyby. Jarndyce appoints Esther as the housekeeper of Bleak House, and although he is old enough to be her father, he entertains thoughts of marrying her. When he finally gets around to asking her, she accepts, but Jarndyce, magnanimous and thoughtful to the last, realizes that she will be much happier with Woodcourt and arranges for that marriage to take place.

Tom Jarndyce

Tom Jarndyce was John Jarndyce's great uncle.

Frustrated at waiting for a judgment in the Jarndyce case, he shot himself. John Jarndyce inherited Bleak House from him.

Caddy Jellyby

Caddy Jellyby is Mrs. Jellyby's oldest daughter. Her mother uses her as a secretary for her philanthropic projects, depriving her of a normal education. She is befriended by Esther, and she marries Prince Turveydrop, ending up managing his dancing academy. She gives birth to a deaf and dumb baby.

Mr. Jellyby

Mr. Jellyby is Mrs. Jellyby's long-suffering husband. A mild-mannered, largely silent man, he goes bankrupt but receives little support from his wife.

Mrs. Jellyby

Mrs. Jellyby is a busy do-gooder who is obsessed with helping the African population of Borrioboola-Gha. She is far more interested in the Africans than she is in her own family, and she neglects her husband and seven children, including her oldest daughter, Caddy.

Peepy Jellyby

Peepy is the youngest Jellyby child. Like all

the others, he is neglected by his mother.

Jenny

Jenny is the wife of a brickmaker in St. Albans. When Esther visits her cottage with Mrs. Pardiggle, Jenny is holding her dead baby. Later, Jenny tries to help Jo. When Lady Dedlock runs away from her home, she stops at Jenny's and changes clothes with her in order to elude pursuit.

Jo

Jo is a boy who ekes out a meager living sweeping a crossing in London. He lives in the slum of Tom-all-Alone's. Most of the time Jo is close to starving; Mr. Snagsby and Nemo take pity on him and are kind to him. After Jo shows Lady Dedlock where Nemo is buried, he attracts the attention of Tulkinghorn and Bucket. Jo catches smallpox, which he passes on to Charley and Esther after they take him to Bleak House. Jo dies at George's shooting gallery, where he has found refuge.

Mr. Kenge

Mr. Kenge is a member of the law firm Kenge and Carboy's, which handles John Jarndyce's affairs. He is called Conversation Kenge because he loves the sound of his own voice.

Mr. Krook

Mr. Krook owns a rag-and-bottle shop that buys up all kinds of junk, including collections of old law documents. The illiterate Krook is an odd, rather sordid old man, "short, cadaverous and withered." His neighbors call him the Lord Chancellor and his shop the Court of Chancery because everything in it is going to ruin. Krook dies when, soaked in alcohol, he spontaneously combusts.

Liz

Liz is a brickmaker's wife and friend of Jenny.

Lord High Chancellor

The Lord High Chancellor presides over the Court of Chancery.

Mercury

Mercury is the footman in the London townhouse of the Dedlocks.

Mr. Neckett

Mr. Neckett, nicknamed Coavinses by Skimpole, is a sheriff's officer who arrests people for debt, including Skimpole. Because of Neckett's occupation, he is unloved. When he dies he leaves three orphans, including Charley.

Charley Neckett

Charley Neckett is the oldest of the three Neckett children. Esther takes her on as a maid. Charley catches smallpox but recovers.

Nemo

Nemo was an army officer, and George served under his command. Captain Hawdon, as he was known in the army, is widely believed to be dead, but in fact, ruined by moneylenders and addicted to opium, he ekes out a living as a law writer who calls himself Nemo. He dies of an overdose of opium, and only gradually does his real identity as Hawdon emerge. He had a love affair with Lady Dedlock before her marriage to Sir Leicester, and this resulted in the birth of Esther.

Mrs. Pardiggle

Mrs. Pardiggle is a tireless woman who likes to think that she is helping the poor when she visits them and gives them lectures, trying to convert them to her religion. She forces her children to donate their allowances to charitable causes, which they bitterly resent.

Rosa

Rosa is a maid at the Dedlock mansion. Lady Dedlock likes her and appoints her as her personal maid in place of Hortense. Rosa is courted by Watt

Rouncewell.

George Rouncewell

See Mr. George

Mr. Rouncewell

Mr. Rouncewell is the successful son of Mrs. Rouncewell. About fifty years old, he is an ironmaster and has been invited to stand for Parliament. He has a confident manner and is not intimidated when he calls on the aristocratic Dedlocks to inform them that his son Watt wishes to marry Rosa.

Mrs. Rouncewell

Mrs. Rouncewell has been housekeeper to the Dedlock family at Chesney Wold for fifty years.

Watt Rouncewell

Watt, Mr. Rouncewell's son, wants to marry Rosa the maid.

Harold Skimpole

Harold Skimpole is a man of about sixty who lives at Bleak House. Skimpole takes pride in describing himself as a child who has no knowledge of financial matters or any sense of responsibility. Because he is charming and entertaining, Skimpole always finds others to support him and pay his bills. Jarndyce, for example, indulges Skimpole's irresponsibility, allowing him to take advantage of his friend's generous spirit. Skimpole is a bad influence on Richard Carstone, and eventually Esther has to tell him to stay away from Richard.

Bart Smallweed

Bart Smallweed is the fifteen-year-old grandson of the Smallweeds. He is a law clerk at Kenge and Carboy.

Judy Smallweed

Judy Smallweed is Bart's twin. She is learning how to make artificial flowers.

Mr. Smallweed

Mr. Smallweed is an old, crippled moneylender. His body is helpless but his mind is sharp, and he takes pleasure in ruining those he lends money to. He traps numerous people, including Hawdon and Mr. George. He is described as "a mere clothes-bag with a black skull-cap on the top of it."

Mrs. Smallweed

Mrs. Smallweed is Mr. Smallweed's wife. He throws pillows at her whenever she mentions the subject of money, which is frequently.

Mr. Snagsby

Mr. Snagsby is the timid owner of the law-stationer's shop in Cook's Court. He is dominated by his shrewish wife.

Mrs. Snagsby

Mrs. Snagsby is the bossy, sharp-tongued wife of Mr. Snagsby. She has a jealous nature and is suspicious when her husband gets caught up in the Lady Dedlock mystery.

Phil Squod

Phil Squod is Mr. George's assistant at the shooting gallery. He used to be a tinker and met with many accidents, as a result of which he is deformed and cannot walk straight.

Esther Summerson

Esther is one of the two narrators of the story. She is raised by her aunt, Miss Barbary, knowing nothing of her parents. Miss Barbary prevents her from mixing with other children, telling her that she is different from them. In spite of her deprived and lonely childhood, however, Esther grows up to be a compassionate, wise, and affectionate young woman, always kind and considerate to others. After her aunt dies, she becomes a schoolteacher and then housekeeper at Bleak House, a position assigned to her by her guardian, John Jarndyce.

Esther eventually discovers that she is the daughter of Lady Dedlock. She catches smallpox as a result of helping Jo, and she is disfigured by the disease. However, this does not prevent her from being courted by Allan Woodcourt, whom she marries. She and Woodcourt settle in a house in Yorkshire that is also called Bleak House.

Mr. Tulkinghorn

Mr. Tulkinghorn is the Dedlocks' lawyer. He is the keeper of all the family secrets, and his loyalty is to Sir Leicester rather than to Lady Dedlock. Tulkinghorn is an austere, detached, remote figure who shows no emotions. He enjoys being in a position of power over others. He is described as "An Oyster of the old school, whom nobody can open."

Mr. Turveydrop

Mr. Turveydrop is Prince's father. He is a vain old man who prides himself on being a model of deportment.

Prince Turveydrop

Prince Turveydrop is a young man who teaches dance. He marries Caddy Jellyby and is a good husband, but his health is poor and he eventually goes lame.

Mr. Vholes

Mr. Vholes is Richard Carstone's lawyer. He is an unpleasant character whose only real purpose is to continue to extract money from Richard.

Mr. Woodcourt

Allan Woodcourt is a doctor, a man of integrity who tries to help the poor, even though he finds it hard to make a living by doing so. He becomes a ship's surgeon in an attempt to improve his financial situation and then becomes a hero when he saves many people after a shipwreck. He marries Esther.

Mrs. Woodcourt

Mrs. Woodcourt is proud of the distinguished Welsh family from whom her son is descended, and at first she opposes a marriage between Allan and Esther because she thinks Esther is not of sufficiently high rank.

Love versus Greed and Self-Interest

For the most part, the characters who embody love and compassion for their fellow humans overcome obstacles and flourish. They are contrasted with those who exist merely to advance their own interests in a greedy fashion, ignoring the needs of others. Esther, for example, is a model of self-effacing goodness, aware of her debt to her guardian and always trying her best, quietly and tactfully, to promote harmony and love. For some readers, Esther may seem too good to be true, a perception that prompted George Orwell to comment facetiously, "it is important to teach boys that women like Esther Summerson don't exist," but Dickens intends her to be a shining light, an example of how simple goodness can triumph in a world full of snares. Esther's eventual husband, Woodcourt, is another example of selflessness; he works to alleviate the suffering of the poor even though he knows he will never get rich by doing so. Mr. George is another example of integrity and compassion; he takes on the deformed Phil Squod as his assistant, thus giving a chance to a man who would otherwise be in desperate straits. He is also willing to take in the unfortunate Jo.

Of the other characters, Ada is unwavering in her selfless devotion to Richard, even though

Richard does little to deserve it, and she eventually finds happiness (one presumes) raising her young son and living with her cousin John Jarndyce. Jarndyce of course is another character whose behavior is impeccable. He always thinks of the welfare of others before his own, and he is willing to make a huge personal sacrifice, renouncing his claim on Esther because he knows she will be happier with Woodcourt.

Topics for Further Study

- One of the most noticeable aspects of *Bleak House* is the vast gap between rich and poor in London. Research the same phenomenon in today's American cities. Why is there such a large gap between rich and poor? What institutions or programs are there to help the poor, and how successful are they? Should the income gap in the United States be reduced or left as it is? If it should be reduced, how can that best be accomplished? Write an essay in which you explore this topic.

- Research traditional beliefs about marriage, the family, and illegitimate births in Western societies. How and why have traditional attitudes changed over the last forty years or so? Are these changes desirable or regrettable? Do children from single-parent families fare as well as those from more traditional family structures? Discuss the topic in an essay.

- Dickens is famous for creating memorable characters. Reread some of his character descriptions in *Bleak House*, such as Mr. Chadband, Inspector Bucket, Boythorn, or any other character who appeals to you. Note the satirical, humorous elements that go into each portrait. Then imagine that you are a modern Dickens and write a paragraph or two in which you describe a character of your own choice. Remember that Dickens, like almost all novelists, often based his characters on real-life people he knew.

- Read Dickens's preface to *Bleak House*, in which he defends the reality of spontaneous human combustion (the fate he gives Krook in the novel). Research spontaneous human combustion on the Internet. Is it a genuine phenomenon or a myth? Give a class presentation on the subject, beginning with the account Dickens gives of Krook's death. Does Dickens's account match other reports of spontaneous human combustion? Can the phenomenon be scientifically proven? If it cannot, what other explanations can be offered for the many stories and examples that testify to it?

Set against these examples of those who are capable of extending themselves beyond their selfish desires are those for whom narrow self-interest and a lack of compassion are the dominating features of their personalities. Many of them have a stake in a corrupt social system, whether financial or legal. Mr. Tulkinghorn, a single man who lives alone and has no family ties, uses his powerful position as a lawyer to exert control over others, regardless of the suffering this may cause. He lives with a closed heart, and his death goes unmourned. Mr. Vholes, Richard Carstone's lawyer, is another example of greed and self-interest. Like Tulkinghorn, he is a serious, self-contained man; he does not reach out to others at a personal level. His only concern is to fulfill the "one great principle of the English law ... to make business for itself" at the expense of his clients. Like others in his profession, Vholes has no regard for morality, for what is right or wrong, but only for what is to his advantage or disadvantage. He may be, in the eyes of society, a "respectable" man, but he is in truth far from it. Not only does his name give his nature away (a vole is a small rodent), but the language with which he is described suggests that he is less than human and has a spooky, ghostlike presence. When Esther meets Vholes, for example, she notes the stark difference between him and her guardian. Whereas Jarndyce speaks openly, Vholes appears to hold in what he has to say in "a cold-blooded, gasping, fish-like manner," and when Vholes leaves, Esther remarks that he "put his dead glove, which scarcely seemed to have any hand in it, on my fingers ... and took his long thin shadow away.... chilling the seed in the ground as it glided along." These descriptions make it clear that Vholes and others like him are scarcely members of the human community. The same applies to the moneylender Smallweed, who is described as resembling a "species of spider" that draws victims into its web, and also, along with the others in his family, as bearing a "likeness to old monkeys." Like his father before him, Smallweed (whose name also gives him away) worships the god of "Compound Interest." He knows how to make money grow, but nothing of what it means to nourish human life.

Families, Orphans, and Abandonment

The ideal presented in the novel is that of the loving family, like the one that Esther finally establishes with Woodcourt and that can also be seen in the Bagnets and, after they have overcome difficulties, the Turveydrops. Many of the families presented are dysfunctional (the Jellybys, the Pardiggles, the Smallweeds) or scattered (the Rouncewells), but Dickens holds up as an ideal the reconciliation and reunion among those who have lost their family connections. Mr. George, for example, is reunited with his mother and his brother after many years of absence, and he finally returns to the house he lived in as a boy to be with his mother. Esther, who thought she was an orphan and was raised in isolation, discovers and is reconciled with her mother. Even though that story ends in tragedy, for Esther finally to meet and forgive her mother is a vital part of her journey of self-discovery and gives her the opportunity to heal some of the wounds of the past.

As Esther's story shows, more characters than not live outside the love and comfort that a family can provide. The shadow cast by those who have in one way or another been abandoned by family or marginalized by society is a long one. These characters are outsiders, struggling to survive as best they can. There is the poor boy Jo, dependent on the kindness of strangers; Miss Flite, whose family has been ruined by the Jarndyce suit and who lives alone at Krook's; Krook himself, origins unknown; Phil Squod, rescued from destitution by George; and Guster, rescued from the workhouse by the Snagsbys. Nemo (Hawdon) is caught in the trap of the moneylenders and lives a shadowy, solitary, anonymous existence; the orphan Charley and her two siblings find their way only through the help of others; and Mr. Gridley is another solitary figure who has lost his family and is driven to distraction and death by a protracted lawsuit. Jarndyce too is alone, although he makes the best of his loneliness through a generous, magnanimous nature.

Of course, having an intact family is no guarantee of love and comfort. Caddy and Peepy Jellyby are virtual orphans even within their own family, so great is their neglect by their mother. Even Ada and Richard, orphans who would appear to be lucky in having the wealthy Jarndyce as their guardian, are made poor by Chancery, which cannot give them their just inheritance. They are orphaned once by death and then again by the legal system.

Given this polarity between the nurturing ideal in a family and the thousand forms in which it breaks down, Dickens appears to put his faith in simple goodness of character that calls some to take care of those who otherwise would be tossed on society's scrap heap. The many who elude this fragile safety net are the nameless multitudes who live and die in urban slums like Tom-all-Alone's, the name itself an apt metaphor for what lies outside the bonds of loving hearth and secure home.

Symbolism

Dickens uses symbolism, a device in which concrete objects are used to represent abstract concepts, in a variety of ways in this novel. He uses the weather, for example, not only to create mood and atmosphere but in a symbolic sense also. The first chapter begins with a long description of the fog in London on a November day. Fog creeps in everywhere, on the river and the marshes, and in the streets, where the stores must light up two hours before darkness falls. The fog is densest around London's legal district: "at the very heart of the fog, sits the Lord High Chancellor in his High Court of Chancery." This august official should be sitting "with a foggy glory round his head." Clearly, fog is a symbol, one might almost say metaphor, for the Court, in which nothing can be seen clearly. People stumble through Chancery without sight of their goal; they wander around, lost and confused.

In chapter II, Dickens also uses the weather to characterize the condition of the Dedlock estate, and the Dedlock family, in Lincolnshire. It has been raining for days. The entire scene is redolent of dreariness and decay. The river is "stagnant," the church in the park is "mouldy," and "there is a general smell and taste as of the ancient Dedlocks in their graves." The dreariness reflects Lady

Dedlock's boredom, and the sense of decay suggests that the fortunes of the family are on their way down. The snowstorm in which Lady Dedlock dies is another symbolic use of the weather. Esther describes how, as she and Bucket search for the runaway woman, "The sleet fell all that day unceasingly, a thick mist came on early, and it never rose or lightened for a moment."

Other symbolic elements include the birds that Miss Flite keeps in cages, which symbolize not only the suitors who are in effect imprisoned by the Jarndyce case but also the various qualities, both good and bad, that the case brings into play. This is shown by the symbolic names she gives the birds (according to Krook in chapter XIII), which include "Hope, Joy, Youth," as well as "Ruin, Despair, Madness, Death," and "Folly, Words, Wigs."

There is a symbolic element also in the description of the environment in which Tulkinghorn lives. On the ceiling of Tulkinghorn's chambers is painted a male figure in a Roman helmet pointing his finger downward. The narrator calls the figure Allegory. Further reference is made to Allegory in chapters XXII and XLII. In the latter, the narrator comments that the room is too dark, even though lit by candles, for Tulkinghorn to see the figure. But after he has had his fateful encounter with Hortense, which will lead to his murder, "now and then, as he throws his head back in his chair, [he catches] sight of the pertinacious Roman pointing from the ceiling." The figure of Allegory, always pointing at the lawyer, is both accuser and prophet of the lawyer's ultimate fate; respectable citizen he may appear to be, but the way he uses his powerful position to manipulate and torment others brings about his inevitable fate. In chapter XLVIII, the narrator draws attention to Allegory pointing down at the corpse of the murdered man.

Finally, Krook's rag-and-bottle shop is a symbolic equivalent of the real nature of the Court of Chancery. Useless stuff accumulates in the shop but nothing ever seems to get sold (just like Chancery in which documents accumulate but there rarely seem to be any judgments). Ironically, although law books and parchment scrolls lie around, Krook is unable to understand any of them because he cannot read. (The lawyers in Chancery can read but they might as well not be able to for all the sense they make.) Krook explains that neighbors have nicknamed him Lord Chancellor and call his shop Chancery because everything in it is "wasting away and going to rack and ruin." Chancery may occupy a fine building, but the dirty, crowded mess that is Krook's shop reveals the true essence of the all-powerful court.

Double Narrative

The novel has two alternating narrators. The first is an almost omniscient narrator who speaks in the third-person voice (using "he" or "she" instead of "I") in the present tense, sometimes called the historic present. This narrator knows about all the events and characters in the story, including their innermost thoughts; he is also what is called an intrusive narrator, in the sense that, as M. H. Abrams puts it, he "comments on his characters, evaluating their actions and motives and expressing his views about human life in general." This is the narrator who adopts a number of different tones throughout the book. He can be sarcastic and ironic (as in his descriptions of Chancery), angry (as in his observations about the life of the poor), and satirical, or lightly mocking (as in his portraits of characters such as Mrs. Jellyby or Mr. Chadband, to name only two). His voice is impersonal; he surveys the scene and makes judgments about it, noting in particular the failures of society's institutions.

In contrast, Esther Summerson tells her story in the first-person voice (using "I"), employing the past tense. This means that she describes only what she personally observes or experiences or hears about from others. Esther's voice is quite different from that of the third-person narrator. Her narrative is marked by her own growing awareness of herself and the world around her. She gradually gets to know about the injustices that the other narrator is always aware of. Her personal voice expresses innocence, faith, goodness, hope, and also common sense, good judgment, and shrewd observation.

Compare & Contrast

- **1850s:** It takes nearly three days to get from Paris to London and then to Lincolnshire in eastern England.

Travelers use a horse and carriage, and cross the English Channel by boat.

Today: Traveling from Paris to London, via the Channel Tunnel, takes only two and a half hours by train, and the drive to Lincolnshire takes only another few hours. By air, it takes one hour to get from Paris to London.

- **1850s:** There is a social stigma attached to having an illegitimate child, a child born out of wedlock. Such children are often given up for adoption.

  Today: The stigma attached to having a child born out of wedlock has largely disappeared, as has the term *illegitimate* in regard to such a child. In the United Kingdom in 2003, 42 percent of children born are born out of wedlock.

- **1850s:** Thousands of poor children in London die young. They live in dirty, cramped conditions, often without heat or adequate food. Only ten years earlier, in 1839, half of all funerals in London were for children under ten years old.

  Today: Although few children in London die of hunger, preventable disease, or neglect, over half a million children in London live in poverty. This represents 41 percent of the total number of children in London.

The Court of Chancery

In Dickens's day, the Court of Chancery was different from the Courts of Common Law. The latter dealt with crimes such as murder and theft, the former with matters such as legacies and trusts. The Court of Chancery was presided over by the Lord Chancellor, the highest legal officer in England. Chancery cases were decided by a judge, not a jury. Cases could drag on for a very long time. Once a case about a disputed will (as in *Bleak House*) was initiated, all property in the case was taken over by the court and was held to ensure that all expenses were met. A long case could mean that the value of the inheritance, once the case was decided, was greatly reduced (to nothing at all in the fictional case of Jarndyce and Jarndyce). Long delays in Chancery were a talking point of the day. In June 1852, for example, the magazine *Punch* discussed a case in which a question of whether an old lady who had died in 1827, twenty-five years earlier ("which is nothing in the age of a Chancery suit"), had made a "power of appointment" in her will. This simple question had involved no fewer than sixteen lawyers, arguing either that she had or had not. Dickens himself was involved in Chancery in 1844 when he sued some publishers for copyright infringement. The ruling was in his favor, but his costs amounted to more than he was able to collect in damages, which contributed to his sour feelings about Chancery proceedings.

Dickens based his tale of Jarndyce and Jarndyce, as he explained in his preface to the novel, on several actual cases, including the Dry case, which began in 1834 and was still continuing, with no sign of a settlement, in 1853, by which time it had already cost more than seventy thousand pounds and involved up to forty lawyers. Dickens also cited a case that had begun in the previous century and was still not resolved but had cost more than twice as much as the Dry case. Bearing these cases in mind, although the Jarndyce and Jarndyce case might seem extreme, scholars are in general agreement that Dickens's portrayal of how the Chancery court operated at the time was accurate.

The British Parliament passed legislation in 1852 that reformed the Court of Chancery. Further reforms followed in 1858 and 1862.

Landowners and Industrialists

The penultimate, or second-to-last, chapter in *Bleak House* shows the decline of the Dedlocks, one of England's great landowning families. The silence at Chesney Wold can be taken at least in part as a metaphor for some of the changes going on in English society during this period. In essence, these upheavals resulted in the strengthening of manufacturing interests at the expense of those of landowners. This was in part a result of the Great Reform Act of 1832, which tripled the number of men allowed to vote in England. The act gave more parliamentary representation to cities, which had grown larger as a result of the Industrial Revolution. This meant that more of the growing middle classes had the opportunity to vote. In 1846, the repeal of the Corn Laws (import tariffs on corn, or grain, that benefited English landowners) was, according to historian George Macauley Trevelyan in his *History of England*, "the first signal victory of the middle classes over the gentry, and of the industrial over the agricultural interest."

This is the background for chapter XL in *Bleak House*. Sir Leicester Dedlock bemoans the emerging political power of industrialists such as Mr. Rouncewell. He is shocked that Mr. Rouncewell, a man of common birth, has been invited to stand for Parliament and has been campaigning against him. In this respect, Sir Leicester appears to have been very much a man of his own time. According to Trevelyan, after the Great Reform Act, and continuing into the 1860s, "the presence on the benches of the House of Commons of persons of middle-class origin … was tolerated as a curiosity or resented as an impertinence by the Whig and Tory squires around them." Sir Leicester is equally shocked when he hears the news that such middle-class upstarts have made gains in the general election of 1852.

The beginning of chapter XL also has contemporary references. Dickens's fictional names Coodle and Doodle represent two great figures in English politics who cannot agree on a government until they realize that the nation is endangered by their disputes. This refers to the instability of the government in 1851 and 1852 and of the party system that produced it. That Coodle and Doodle finally reach agreement is likely a reference to the formation of a coalition government under Lord Aberdeen in 1853. But Dickens was obviously not impressed by this compromise and attacked the prevalence of bribery in the political process. He presents a picture of "Britannia being much occupied in pocketing Doodle in the form of sovereigns, and swallowing Doodle in the form of beer, and in swearing herself black in the face that she does neither." He was not alone in bringing attention to these abuses. In 1852, the town of St. Albans, which figures prominently in *Bleak House*, was disenfranchised, that is, taken off the election rolls, by act of Parliament because of bribery and corruption. The Corrupt Practices at Elections Act, also passed in 1852, further focused attention on the issue of political bribery.

Critical Overview

Reviews of *Bleak House* after the publication of the final installment in 1853 were mixed. Some reviewers found it too full of unsympathetic characters and lacking in humor, although characters such as Jo and Inspector Bucket were widely admired. Some special interests were offended by Dickens's satires of various social groups: politically, Conservatives objected to the portrayal of Sir Leicester Dedlock, while Liberals and feminists took issue with the presentation of Mrs. Jellyby. The satirical portrait of Chadband, the pompous preacher, also aroused indignation in some religious circles. Among literary critics, George Brimley, in *Spectator*, criticized the novel for a lacking a coherent plot. He comments, "The series of incidents which form the outward life of the actors and talkers has no close and necessary connexion"; he adds that the Chancery suit "has positively not the smallest influence on the character of any one person concerned; nor has it any interest of itself." A much more positive view was taken by Dickens's friend, John Forster, in his unsigned review in *Examiner*. Forster writes that the novel "touches and amuses us, but it is destined to draw tears and smiles also from our children's children." Forster had particular praise for the characters Mrs. Jellyby, Boythorn, Skimpole, and Chadband, as part of "that crowd of fresh and ever real creations that will live while the language continues."

From the 1850s to the 1870s, *Bleak House* was regarded by many critics as falling far short of Dickens's best work, but this is a view that modern critics have not shared. In fact, over the last half century, the standing of the novel has steadily increased. In 1964, Geoffrey Tillotson called the novel "the finest literary work the nineteenth century produced in England," as quoted by Elliot L. Gilbert in the introduction to *Critical Essays on Charles Dickens's "Bleak House."* Gilbert offers an explanation of why *Bleak House* has recently attracted as much or more critical attention than any other work by Dickens. He suggests that in the novel, the "freshness and spontaneity" of Dickens's early works combine with the "deliberate structuring and complex thematic development" of the later books in "a perfect balance." In the introduction to a Modern Critical Interpretations edition of the novel, renowned critic Harold Bloom praises the character of Esther as "the most mysteriously complex and profound personage" in the novel and comments that "there is now something close to critical agreement that *Bleak House* is Dickens's most complex and memorable single achievement."

What Do I Read Next?

- Dickens's novel *Hard Times* (first published in 1854 and available in several modern editions) is one of Dickens's shorter novels. It is set in the fictional northern industrial city of Coketown and includes Dickens's satire of the English educational system, which emphasizes the learning of facts and discourages the development of the imagination. Dickens also targets the utilitarians, who see everything in terms of facts, figures, and statistics, and calls for an improvement in working conditions in factories.

- *Vanity Fair: A Novel Without a Hero* by William Makepeace Thackeray was first published in serial form between 1847 and 1848. One of the great Victorian novels, it is set a generation earlier than *Bleak House*, in early nineteenth-century England, and is a satire on the hypocrisy of English society. A modern edition was published in 2003 in the Penguin Classics series.

- *North and South* by Elizabeth Gaskell was first published in *Household Words*, the magazine edited by Dickens, in weekly installments from 1854 to 1855. The novel, which is considered to be Gaskell's best, describes the life of a young woman who moves from a prosperous but boring life in southern England to the industrial north. She learns there about the hardships endured by factory workers and also develops a romantic interest in a mill owner. The novel conveys much about industrial conditions in England in the mid-nineteenth century as well as relations between men and women at the time.

- *Dickens: A Biography* (1988) by Fred Kaplan is well regarded for its meticulous research and fair-minded judgments. It is also highly readable and was named as a notable book of the year by the *New York Times*. In a swift-moving narrative, Kaplan brings out some of the contradictions and conflicts in Dickens's personality as he describes the novelist's successful career, his wide circle of friends, and his unhappy marriage.

Sources

Abrams, M. H., *A Glossary of Literary Terms*, 4th ed., Holt, Rinehart and Winston, 1981, p. 143.

Ackroyd, Peter, *Dickens*, Mandarin, 1991, pp. 405-406.

Allen, Tim, "15 May 2006: International Day of Families: The Family in the EU25 Seen Through Figures," in *Europa*, May 12, 2006, http://europa.eu (accessed October 11, 2008).

Bloom, Harold, "Introduction," in *Charles Dickens's "Bleak House," Modern Critical Interpretations*, edited by Harold Bloom, Chelsea House, 1987, pp. 5, 6.

Brimley, George, Review of *Bleak House*, in *Dickens: The Critical Heritage*, edited by Philip Collins, Routledge and Kegan Paul, 1971, p. 283; originally published in *Spectator*, September 24, 1853, pp. 923-25.

"A Chancery Bone of Contention," in *Charles Dickens, "Bleak House,"* Norton Critical Edition, edited by George Ford and Sylvère Monod, W. W. Norton, 1977, p. 924; originally published in *Punch*, Vol. 22, June 1852, p. 255.

Dickens, Charles, *Bleak House*, Oxford Illustrated Dickens, Oxford University Press, 1996.

Disraeli, Benjamin, *Sybil: Or the Two Nations*, Penguin Books, 1985, p. 96; originally published

1845.

Forster, John, Review of *Bleak House*, in *Dickens: The Critical Heritage*, edited by Philip Collins, Routledge and Kegan Paul, 1971, pp, 290, 292; originally published in *Examiner*, October 8, 1853, pp. 643-45.

Gilbert, Elliot L., "Introduction," in *Critical Essays on Charles Dickens's "Bleak House,"* G. K. Hall, 1989, p. 1.

London Child Poverty Commission Web site, http://213.86.122.139 (accessed October 11, 2008).

Mayhew, Henry, *London Labour and the London Poor*, selections and introduction by Victor Neuberg, Penguin Books, 1985, p. 257.

Orwell, George, *The Collected Essays, Journalism and Letters of George Orwell*, edited by Sonia Orwell and Ian Angus, Vol. 1, Penguin Books, 1970, p. 50.

Shatto, Susan, *The Companion to "Bleak House,"* Unwin Hyman, 1988, p. 114.

Trevelyan, George Macauley, *History of England*, Longmans, Green, 1929, pp. 644, 646.

Further Reading

Hawthorn, Jeremy, *Bleak House*, Macmillan, 1987.

> Hawthorn describes the range of critical approaches to *Bleak House*: as an anatomy of society, in terms of narrative and form, feminist responses, and studies of character. In the second part of the book, Hawthorn discusses the experience readers go through as they read the novel.

Korg, Jacob, ed., *Twentieth Century Interpretations of* Bleak House: *A Collection of Critical Essays*, Prentice-Hall, 1968.

> This selection of essays contains some of the best studies of *Bleak House* from the 1950s and 1960s. The essay by J. Hillis Miller in particular is now regarded as a classic piece of criticism.

Leapman, Michael, *The World for a Shilling: How the Great Exhibition of 1851 Shaped a Nation*, Headline Book Publishing, 2002.

> The Great Exhibition, aimed at showing off Victorian industrial technology and design, was held in London in 1851. It was visited by six million people, a quarter of the

population of Britain. Leapman shows how the exhibition was planned and created and how it excited the imagination of the British public. His account reveals much about the confidence, optimism, and inventiveness of the early Victorian era, the period in which *Bleak House* is set.

Paterson, Michael, *Voices from Dickens' London*, 2nd ed., David & Charles PLC, 2007.

This work offers a glimpse into all aspects of nineteenth-century London through the accounts of residents of and visitors to the city in letters, diaries, and newspapers, as well as some of Dickens's own writings. The book reveals how difficult and even brutal life was for the majority of people in this huge city at a time of great growth and change.